Plain  Traditions:
Amish & Mennonite Holidays

By Sarah Price

This book or parts thereof may not be reproduced in any form, stored in a retrieval system, or transmitted in any form by any means—electronic, mechanical, photocopy, recording, or otherwise—without prior written permission of the publisher, except as provided by United States of America copyright law.

Copyright © 2014 by Price Publishing, LLC.
All rights reserved.

Cover design by
Dutch Valley Tech and used with permission.

Photo credits of farm by Destination Amish
Copyright © 2014
Used with permission.

DEDICATION

Dedicated to my grandmother, Sarah Marie Alderfer, for all of our letters, talks, and time shared debating cultural and religious topics. You remain my best friend and the motivation for much of my writing. You are greatly missed.

Dedicated to my parents, Stanley Alderfer Nice and Eleanor Hale Nice, for all of their encouragement, love, and support over the years.

DEDICATION	**3**
ACKNOWLEDGMENTS	**9**
Foreword	11
A Prayer of Thanks	15
Introduction	17
A Holiday Devotion	21
Christmas Memories	23
My Christmas Wish	29
Plain & Simple Decorating	31
Traditions	35
Amish Traditions	35
Mennonite Traditions	40
Favorite Hymns	47
Good Christian Men, Rejoice!	48
The Happy Morn	49
The Herald Angels	51
The First Noël	53
Silent Night	55
RecipeS	57
Essential Ingredients	57
Other Essential Items	58
Beverages & Punch	61
Basic Punch	62
Cranberry Punch	63
Egg Nog	64

Momma Dee's Ski Tea	65
Root Beer	66
Breakfast Treats	**67**
Baked Omelet	68
Cheesy Breakfast Casserole	69
Hash Browns	70
Baked Potato Cakes	71
Waffles	72
Breads	**73**
Basic Bread Recipe	74
Basic Croissant Rolls	76
Basic Dinner Rolls	78
Blueberry Muffins	79
Cinnamon Crescent Roll	81
Pumpkin Muffins	82
Zucchini Bread	84
Starters	**87**
Apple and Cheese Dip	88
Cup Cheese	89
Deviled Eggs	90
Ham Balls	92
Micheline Salad	94
Soups	**97**
Basic Amish Soup	98
Chicken Corn Soup	99

Chicken Noodle Soup	101
Cream of Mushroom Soup	102
Oyster Stew	104
Potato Soup	106

Main Dishes — 107

Bacon, Lettuce, Tomato Sandwich	108
Baked Ham	110
Chicken Pot Pie	111
Chicken, Roasted	113
Ham Loaf	114
Roasted Turkey	115
Lasagna	116
Meatballs	118
Meatloaf Surprise	119
Sausage and Sauerkraut	121
Shepherd's Pie	122
Workday Dinner	123

Side Dishes: Vegetables & Others — 125

Applesauce	126
Baked Corn	127
Carrot Casserole	128
Green Bean Casserole	129
Maple Syrup Carrots	130
Mashed Turnips	131
Sweet and Sour Green Beans	132

Side Dishes: Starches — 133

    Amish Casserole — 134
    Baked Macaroni and Cheese — 136
    Broccoli Casserole — 138
    Candied Sweet Potatoes — 140
    Pennsylvania Dutch Corn Pie — 141
    Lisa's Sweet Potato Casserole — 143
    Mother-In-Law's Rice Casserole — 145
    Mashed Potatoes — 146
    Oyster Stuffing — 148
    Roasted Butternut Squash — 150

Pickled Dishes & Relishes — 151

    Amish Chow Chow — 152
    Pickled Beets — 154
    Pickled Cabbage — 155
    Pickled Eggs — 157
    Refrigerator Pickles — 158

Desserts — 159

    Basic Pie Crust — 160
    Applesauce Cake — 161
    Black Walnut Layer Cake — 162
    Buttercream Icing — 164
    Funny Cake — 165
    Ground Cherry Pie — 167
    Pecan Pie — 169

Pretzel Salad	171
Shoo-fly Pie	173
Snitz Pie	174
Weekly Recipes	**175**
Want to Contribute?	**176**
ABOUT THE AUTHOR	**178**

ACKNOWLEDGMENTS

No book is ever written by one author. It takes a team of people to write a book. Without the help of Lisa Bull, Dutch Valley Tech, and my wonderful editing team, this book would not have happened.

I also thank my friend, Judy Keller, for helping me understand the proper processing for canning food! Her knowledge is invaluable. <3

FOREWORD

My grandmother, Sarah Marie, was born in the early 1900s to a Mennonite family in Harleysville, Pennsylvania.

She had three siblings, two brothers and a much younger sister, Mildred. When my grandmother married Harlan Nice, he was a bit of a rebel by Mennonite standards. He bought a car before anyone else in the church district and, as the story is often told, was brought before the church leaders on more than one occasion for being too worldly. Each time, he managed to talk his way out of being shunned.

What led my grandmother to be attracted to such a rebel will never be known…the secrets reside in their graves. But, knowing my grandmother, she felt a tenderness for the young man who lost his mother and sister during the influenza pandemic in 1919. While Harlan was raised in a very strict Mennonite household, he also managed to charm his way out of many situations.

Looking back, I learned a lot from my grandparents: patience, independence, loyalty, and honesty. I also learned to respect my heritage, ancestors who gave up so much in order to ensure that their children and grandchildren, and great-grandchildren could worship God without fear of persecution.

After my grandfather passed away, my grandmother and I became the best of friends. I would visit her every Friday, even when I had to drag a small baby with me for the three hour drive there and back. It was worth it to see her smile.

The holidays have never quite been the same since

my grandparents joined Jesus in heaven. The simple meals, usually served in the basement of their house with multiple tables lined up and covered with different table linens, seemed to taste different from what foods we serve at our Christmas gatherings today. Maybe it's the fact that our meals are no longer plain and simple. Or maybe it's that they just do not have the history of being passed down from generation to generation.

Either way, the holidays are a lot different now. But my memories recall the sounds, smells, and feelings that surrounded that table in the basement of their ranch house in Harleysville, Pennsylvania. Perhaps one day we will be able to return to simpler times. If not, however, I sure do hope that this book helps people see that plain and simple is easier to do (and just as tasty!) as rich and fancy.

For just a few moments, step back in time with me to the 1960s and 1970s when Christmas was less about commercialism and more about the holy aspect of the holiday.

~Sarah Price

A PRAYER OF THANKS

by Lisa Bull

Father,

We come to You today, with thankfulness in our hearts.
Thank You for the sacrifice of Your Son.
Thank You that all we have to do is call on
His name to have freedom in You.

Thank You for providing financially for those who are struggling.
Thank You for healing those who are sick.
Thank You for mending broken relationships.
Thank You for touching confused minds and restoring clarity.
Thank You for piecing back together the broken-hearted.
Thank You for Your protection.
Thank You for Your Peace.
You are a good God, worthy of our praise and thanksgiving.

Amen.

Growing fields and rolling hills. An Amish farm in Holmes County Ohio is breathtaking, for sure and certain. A special thank you to Destination Amish for granting permission to use this photograph.

INTRODUCTION

One of my earliest memories is visiting my grandparents' house in Pennsylvania. They lived in a stone ranch house that my grandfather built on a small piece of property adjacent to my great-grandparents' farm.

Their house always smelled like good food, the kitchen being in the center of the house and my grandmother almost always cooking. By comparison with other Mennonite families in the 1950s and 1960s, their home and kitchen was smaller than others. My grandparents only had four children and eight grandchildren. Still, with the exception on one aunt, the rest of the family never moved far away so someone was always visiting with my grandparents.

At the time, my family lived around the corner from their house. Visiting my grandparents was an almost a daily occurrence. Behind our house was a great big field across which we would walk in order to reach my grandparents' house. My grandmother would wait at the edge of her yard and, when we approached, she would cross the road to fetch us.

Inside the house, there would be freshly baked sugar cookies or brownies. She always had freshly washed and cut grapes in the refrigerator and a pitcher of iced tea made from mint she grew in her garden. If the weather was cold, we might even get hot chocolate with little marshmallows floating on the top.

As the youngest of the grandchildren, I was often left behind when my cousins were there. Maybe that was the reason why I developed such a close relationship with both my grandfather and my grandmother.

I remember sitting on my grandfather's lap while my grandmother cooked supper (which, by the way, always included mashed potatoes!). He would clutch his black leather Bible in his hand, but he never referenced it: He knew Scripture by heart.

Years later, after my grandmother passed away, I found that worn Bible, along with my grandmother's and my great-grandfather's, in the garbage. I was not too proud to jump into the dumpster and rescue them. Today, those Bibles sit on the shelves in my downstairs library and I often pull them down to leaf through the old pages, noting the different underlined verses and comments written in the margins.

The one verse that I have never forgotten is the most important one in the Bible:

> For God so loved the world that he gave his one and only Son, that whoever believes in him shall not perish but have eternal life. For God did not send his Son into the world to condemn the world, but to save the world through him.
> John 3:16 (KJV)

For me, and millions of other Christians, this is the true meaning of Christmas: the celebration of an incredible act of love offered by God to you and me.

Out of gratitude for this amazing gift, given to us by God, Christmas has become a day to remember the birth of Jesus Christ.

Throughout the years, this holy day has slowly morphed into something very different. In addition to worshipping Him, we exchange gifts with our family and friends. We also become more reflective on how fortunate we are and how others are not.

As I get older, I notice that more and more people do not understand the true meaning of Christmas. It's hard to remember when we are bombarded with so much commercialism. Between advertisements for every gadget under the sun and sales that start even before Thanksgiving, the focus seems to drift away from God's gift of love and toward mankind's love of gifts.

This year, I want to focus on the true meaning of

Christmas and not the commercial one. I want a return to the plain and simple traditions that my dear Amish friends and Mennonite family exhibit.

I'm so glad that you decided to join me on this journey. God's gift is the only one that we truly need.

Blessings,
Sarah Price
sarahprice.author@gmail.com
http://www.facebook.com/fansofsarahprice
Twitter: @SarahPriceAuthr

A HOLIDAY DEVOTION

By Lisa Bull

Today begins Thanksgiving week. A week during which we, as a country, reflect on the Pilgrims who sacrificed their lives in the hope of freedom to worship. They gave up everything they knew for the unknown, trusting for something better. Had it not been for their sacrifice, their bravery...well...have you ever wondered what a different world this would be?

They gave everything, in faith, believing God would provide.

Do you have that kind of faith? That same spirit/ Do you believe God can and will provide for your every need? Do you thank Him for what He has done? His goodness is, indeed, all around. Do you take the time to notice?

Psalm 95:1-6
King James Version

1 O come, let us sing unto the Lord: let us make a joyful noise to the rock of our salvation.

> 2 Let us come before his presence with thanksgiving, and make a joyful noise unto him with psalms.
>
> 3 For the Lord is a great God, and a great King above all gods.
>
> 4 In his hand are the deep places of the earth: the strength of the hills is his also.
>
> 5 The sea is his, and he made it: and his hands formed the dry land.
>
> 6 O come, let us worship and bow down: let us kneel before the Lord our maker.

God created the Heavens and the Earth. He knows every galaxy and He sees the very core of the earth. He knows every living thing from the largest to the smallest, even in the deepest darkest part of the sea. He commands the sun to rise and the moon to shine. He takes care to feed the smallest of birds and dresses the fields with flowers. Don't you think you can trust Him with your life?

The Pilgrims sacrificed everything, ultimately giving us the country that we now call home.

God sacrificed His only Son so that we could have freedom in our hearts and, in the end, an eternal home with Him. Doesn't that deserve Thanksgiving?

There are so many things to be thankful for this week, and every week. Take time to be grateful.

CHRISTMAS MEMORIES

By Eleanor Nice

The memories that we make today often become the traditions of tomorrow within our families. By the word's definition, we know that traditions are the long-established customs that pass from one generation to the next, the very glue which holds families together. Since traditions define the family and make it special, their expectancy and the familiarity makes traditions themselves part of the holidays.

As I was growing up, my father struggled to put food on the table. It was just the two of us and my father worked long hours, week after week. During Christmas, we focused on spending time together, often taking one night before the holiday to drive to Bethlehem, Pennsylvania so we could sit in his beat up old green Ford pickup to look at the big star that they townspeople lit up on the large hill.

Throughout the year, my father had one passion and that was playing the organ. After a long day working at his father's service station, the very first one in Philadelphia, he would practice for hours. The only problem was that he knew just one song: Silent Night. Over and over, my father would play Silent Night and sing as loud as he could.

When Christmas came, he would play this song for anyone and everyone who visited our small house in Plymouth Meeting. It was a tradition that people knew came to expect upon entering through the front door. And, for the most part, no one minded the fact that he sang off key or hit the wrong notes because he sang with all of his heart. The joy on his face was overwhelming and put everyone into the Christmas spirit.

Still, traditions change over time.

Since my father's passing, I cannot listen to Silent Night without crying, remembering those organ notes resonating in our house and through my heart.

Other traditions replace the old ones.

When our grandchildren were little, I started a new tradition called "Find the Pickle". Each year, we hid one little green pickle ornament on the Christmas tree. The grandchildren have to find the pickle in order to win a candy cane. Sometimes even the adults cannot find it! But we had fun standing around the tree looking for it.

One tradition that we can count on is that my daughter, Sarah, will always try to do something special for us. She likes change so she often comes up with new, creative ways to show her love for the family.

One Christmas morning, Sarah arranged for her husband, Marc, to pick us up with a horse-drawn carriage. With sleigh bells on the back and a blanket to snuggle under, we rode around the neighborhood. It was a picture perfect scene. People waved from passing cars, and neighbors came out to enjoy the wonderful sigh of the majestic horse and beautiful carriage.

The lesson here is to do something special for other people during this joyous time of year.

- Leave cookies at a neighbor's door.
- Tie a ribbon on a friend's mailbox.
- Give food to a food bank or at church for the food drive.
- Say a special prayer for those in need.
- Sing a Christmas carol with your children and grandchildren.

Increasingly, as Sarah often points out, it is apparent that Christmas can get out of hand and there is too much emphasis on gifts and trees, decorations and trimming. It's almost a contest as to who will spend the most on Christmas decor!

We are all guilty of doing too much, especially my

daughter. Admittedly, she takes after her mother, which, on most days, makes me rather happy, I'll admit.

This year, Sarah's emphasis is on keeping the focus on the birth of Jesus Christ and all of its meaning. We often say that we want to cut back and focus on the *holy* part of the holiday. This year, we will. After all, it is up to us to keep it in perspective.

Whatever you like is what you should continue to do. Don't get bogged down with the mundane things. Instead, focus on what you can do with what you have. If your Christmas cards don't get sent out, use social media. If you have limited ability to buy gifts, considering baking a cake or cupcakes. Gifts don't have to come from Sears or Macy's to be priceless.

At home, you can make it festive without breaking the bank: hang up the Christmas cards, put simple greens around the house, place a wreath on your front door, hang a swag of greens with a pretty bow on your mailbox.

Maybe all of the above is still too much. Then visit a church and say a prayer for better days. Those doors are always open and the poinsettias will be something beautiful for you to enjoy.

One doesn't not have to be rich to experience Christmas.

This is the one day per year when people are the kindest and the friendliest. Let's try to keep that attitude for all 364 days until next year.

MERRY CHRISTMAS TO ALL!

May your happy traditions continue whether you are Amish, Mennonite or Christian. We are all God's children.

One of the most fascinating things about Amish farms is how clean and tidy they are usually kept. Just as they practice in their religion and life, they keep their homes plain and simple, too. Everything has a purpose and is reused (if possible).

This photograph was taken by Destination Amish and used with their permission.

MY CHRISTMAS WISH

By Sarah Price

It's important to remember that Christmas is not about spending money or buying gifts. It's about experiencing the joy of the people that we love: family, friends, even colleagues. It is about the time of finding the good in people, even those who did not always do right by us in the past.

This Christmas, I intend to focus on the simpler things in life: the joy of gathering together (and not just for giving). My tree is a simple branch on a round table with envelopes that contain promises to the recipients…promises to spend more time, to do more good, and to laugh more often with each person. There is no price that we can we put on *those* gifts; yet, they are the most special gifts of all.

Even more importantly, I have a selfish Christmas wish…that people give the gift of considering other before they think of themselves.

- To give without expecting anything in receipt.
- To show kindness even when there is no chance of gratitude.
- To show gratitude whenever there is a hint of

kindness.

- To speak with a soft tongue and considerate heart so other people are not injured by harsh or selfish words.
- To refrain from retaliating when people speak in a cruel and heartless manner.
- To use the word "you" more than the word "I."

Maybe that's an awful lot to ask, but that is my Christmas wish. The down side to these wishes, of course, is that in order to gift them to others, that means others are most likely not giving them back to you.

If you think about Jesus and the sacrifices that He made, did he not offer these gifts to mankind? He gave without expecting anything in return. He showed kindness which was not appreciated by the masses. He demonstrated gratitude for the small things that we might normally take for granted. And He refrained from speaking out against those that wanted to harm Him.

Among many other things, those were gifts that He gave to us. Mayhaps it's time for us to give those gifts back to the people that surround us in order to spread Christmas cheer and the love of Jesus.

PLAIN & SIMPLE DECORATING

Both the Amish and the Mennonite place little emphasis on holiday decorations. There are no Christmas trees, lighted bushes, or even battery-operated candles in the windows.

Their emphasis is on the birth of Jesus Christ.

That being said, they have a wonderful way of making their homes feel special for the holidays. The following are some fun and simple decorating ideas that come directly from my Amish friends and Mennonite family:

- Tie a string from one end of the room to another and hang your Christmas cards over them (as if on a clothes line). The festive photos will brighten any room.
- Cut old Christmas cards into small squares (4x4 or 3x4). Glue them back to back and then punch holes along one edge. Tie the holes with festive yarn to make Christmas photo books for children that come visiting. Also works great in church to occupy restless grandchildren.
- Using old Christmas cards, punch holes in pretty patterns in them as well as along the

edges. Use red yarn to tie them together in the shape of a house (five rectangular shapes for two long walls, floor, and the two peaked roof pieces—and two squares with points for the sides). Place a battery operated tea light inside the house.

HINT: Make a pattern on construction paper and keep it for future use.

- Using the above Christmas card house, fill it with Hershey kisses and give it as a hostess gift when visiting friends.
- Take a glass bowl, put a white candle (real or battery operated) into the center, and surrounded with red marbles. Set it on your kitchen table for a festive look.
- Cut off lower branches of an evergreen tree, tie them together, and place on window ledges (more appropriate with wider window sills).
- Purchase an old fashion lantern and fill it with red lantern oil. Be certain to purchase extra wicks. For an extra pretty flame, snip the edges of the wick with scissors so that the center is angled up in a point.
- Put out glass bowls with individually wrapped red candies. Besides looking pretty, the sweets will be appreciated by your guests.

- Hang bright red scarves on your coat rack (or hooks near the door). The color will brighten the entrance while being convenient to use when running out the door on cold, winter days.

There are many ways to decorate your home during the Christmas season without spending too much money. Focusing on the true reason of the holiday, is the best way to keep it plain and simple while creating memories that last a lifetime.

The Alderfer family in an undated photo from the collection of Sarah Price.

An old photograph of my great-grandparents and other family members. The older generation is much more conservative than the younger generation (see young lady on the left). My Mennonite ancestors came over to America in 1705 to escape persecution. Over the years, they help onto their conservative beliefs. However, you can see from this photograph that change was in the air. Unlike the Amish, the Mennonites allow photo taking. I'm fortunate to have found my grandmother's collection before it was discarded after she passed away. ~Sarah

TRADITIONS

AMISH TRADITIONS

The Christmas celebration among the Amish is different from the way that non-Amish celebrate the birth of Jesus Christ.

As you read above, holiday decorations are very low-key. Presents are kept to a minimum. Families will gather together, not always on Christmas Day.

In fact, readers might find it hard to believe that the Amish do not even attend church on Sunday unless Christmas falls on a Sunday. The host family would have too much pressure preparing for preparing family meals to celebrate Christmas while also getting the house ready for a worship service.

In the case of Sunday falling on the actual date of Christmas (or December 26 which the Amish also use for visiting family and feasting), the bishop might cancel that service or the entire g'may, or church district, will help prepare the house and the meals so that the burden is not on the hostess.

The service before (or immediately after) Christmas is a regular service. There is no Christmas tree, candles, or gift exchanging. The sermon may (but also may not) focus on the birth of Jesus. It is, in fact, a regular worship service.

In regard to the family gatherings, each family will host one gathering in their house—if it is large enough to host upwards of fifty people. Since older children have families of their own, not all of the children will be present, but they will make a special trip to share fellowship with their parents on another occasion, if possible.

During the main meal (usually early afternoon so that families can return to their homes for chores), they will sing hymns from the Ausbund in German as well as some hymns in English such as Silent Night. Singing is a big part of their gatherings, whether birthdays, anniversaries, or Christmas. The sound of fifty voices rising up in harmony, no music to accompany them, is truly a memory I will never forget and one that I wish I could personally share with each and every reader.

As for gifts, grandparents and parents will gift their smaller children one item and it is usually something small and useful: a handmade scarf, new mittens, perhaps a wooden toy. One Amish woman that I am friends with makes little houses out of old Christmas cards, holes punched in cute patterns along the sides, and puts a battery operated candle in the house so that, at night, it shines through the punched holes.

Another Amish woman likes to visit garage sales during the summer months and purchase "dolls" to give to her smaller nieces and nephews. She will wrap them in hand-knit blankets.

One time I asked my Amish friend if she ever gave a present to her mother. She thought for a moment and then gasped. "Why I don't think us children ever did!"

Another Christmas, my Amish friend set out three lap blankets she had crocheted. She asked me which one I liked the best. When I pointed out the one with the amazing pattern, a zig-zag pattern, she smiled and said, "That is your Christmas present from me, then."

I've noticed that gift giving among adults is not as popular; the emphasis is more on sharing time together. But when they do give gifts, a lot of times it is either something they made or something with a story behind it. My younger Amish friend gave me her mother's kerosene lantern. They used battery operated lanterns since their children were smaller and she said that she couldn't think of anyone who would love the kerosene lantern more than I would.

Recycling gifts is not uncommon. In fact, it seems to give them the greatest joy. They put thought into who would like a particular item that they no longer use: a platter, a set of Tupperware, an old quilt, a book of devotions. They are giving people, but the gifts come when they want to give them and not just at Christmas. In fact, Christmas gifts are truly kept to a minimum.

One gift that every community enjoys is the annual Christmas pageant at the local schoolhouse. The children will sing songs, quote Bible verses, and, in some less conservative g'mays retell the story of the nativity. The teacher might have the windows decorated with a simple branch from a pine tree and battery operated candles might adorn windowsills.

Children may receive a small gift from the teacher such as a pencil or eraser, something of use. More importantly, the children may have worked together to make gifts for people within their g'may, such as a book of handwritten verses or colored pictures to give to someone who may have lost a loved one recently.

Those small schoolhouses have standing room only since parents, grandparents, and siblings will attend. It's also a chance for a young man to escort a young woman home in his buggy.

Another tradition that might come as a surprise to many readers is that the Amish really celebrate the religious aspects of Christmas on January 6th. They call it Old Christmas. Businesses are closed and families gather once again for feasting and fellowship. There are no gifts exchanged.

The biggest Christmas tradition among the Amish is being together and enjoying each others' company. It isn't about the biggest tree or prettiest decoration. It isn't about lovely wrapped gifts or fancy table settings. Just like the Amish, they keep it plain and simple…and focus on what is truly important: God's gift to mankind…His son.

MENNONITE TRADITIONS

An undated photograph of the Alderfer home in Harleysville from the collection of Sarah Price.

This was the small house that my great-grandparents lived in and raised their children. My grandmother, Sarah Marie, lived here with her husband, Harlan Nice, when they were first married. Three of her four children were born in this house.

Years later, Harlan (or PopPop as I called him), bought a piece of land, adjacent to this farm, from my great-grandfather. Harlan built a lovely little ranch house. It's still there today on Broad Street in Harleysville.

My family spent many holidays at this house as well as the ranch house. Our tradition was to gather in the basement at a long set of tables covered with different colored tablecloths for our meal.

An undated photograph of a Mennonite table ready for fellowship from the collection of Sarah Price.

Since the Amish do not allow photographs, I can only share some photographs that I found from the boxes held by my grandparents. Like the Amish, my grandmother did not decorate the house with trees or garland. There were no crosses or statues of Jesus, not even nativity sets. After all, one of the commandments instructs His followers to make no engraved images. Ironically, the Mennonites (and some Amish) do allow photographs. I've never been quite sure about why the Mennonites are so accepting of photographs while most Amish are against it. I suspect it has more to do with pride, besides the commandment from God—that's just my opinion, though.

Although the previous photograph was clearly not taken at Christmas, this is a typical set up for both Amish and Mennonite gatherings. Tables are set up (outside in nice weather, inside in colder seasons) with a mix-match of tablecloths and a smorgasbord of food. Paper plates might be used or, more likely, families will bring their own flatware, all marked on the back with their initials or name, written in permanent black marker.

With the Mennonites, at least in our family, the children always sat at one end and the adults at the other. As the youngest child, I never made it to the adult table, something which my cousins and sister liked to tease me about for years.

Unlike the Amish, the Mennonites pray out loud. My grandfather always gave the most wonderful blessings over the food and the people gathered both around the table and in our hearts. He always prayed for the poor and the needy. His final prayer was that the lost would be saved.

When the meal was served, there would be so much food on the table and most of the recipes are on the following pages of this books. We always had roasted turkey, mashed potatoes (two bowls: one for me, one for everyone else), pickled cabbage, oyster stuffing, applesauce, green bean casserole, maple syrup carrots, and desserts that would just make you regret having eaten so much beforehand!

After everyone's belly was full and the women had cleaned the dishes, a rapid chore with so many hands to help, we would gather around my grandmother's piano and sing Christmas hymns. My grandmother loved that piano and played hymns as often as she could. At Christmas time, she loved to play songs about baby Jesus and the wise men. We would stand around and sing, some of us needing a little guidance with the words and quite a few of us needing help carrying a tune.

We would exchange gifts later. Gathered in the living room, the adults on the sofa and folding chairs with the younger children seated on the floor, we would anxiously await the gifts from our dear Pop-Pop and Mom-Mom.

One gift. One very special gift that always had the exact same value. If there was a difference in the value of the gift, that extra money would be put in an envelope for that person. Above all else, they wanted to be fair.

For the men, they could count on a new pair of black socks, usually in a package of three. For the women, my grandmother always did a grab-bag. During the year, she would visit garage sales and find pretty dishes or tea cups. At Christmas, she would wrap them up and put them in a plain box. My aunts and my mother would pick a wrapped gift and open it. It was the funnest part of the gift giving.

One year, my Pop-Pop wanted my mother to have a special one of those grab bag gifts and he nudged it closer to her and gave her a special wink. It was a beautiful teapot with a floral design on the side and gold on the handle. That was the only time I ever witnessed a little favoritism. The memory warms my heart because he was truly a kind hearted, generous man and if he wanted my mother to have that teapot, there was a reason that only he knows but surely it was a good one.

For the grandchildren, the boys usually received socks and the girls a similar grab bag gift like the older women. For me, however, they always had something special. I was a lot younger than the other cousins and, being known as a reader, it was not unusual to have a book as my gift. But always, whatever the gift was, my grandparents ensured that they were all of equal value.

I miss those holiday gatherings. Ever since my grandmother passed away, it seems the family doesn't gather anymore. I miss the simple decorations, the different dishes of food, the laughter of my aunts, and the gentle ribbing the cousins give each other over how much older they are now...some with grandchildren!

Traditions change with time, I suppose.

PRICE

FAVORITE HYMNS

No Christmas gather is complete without the gift of song. While the Amish and most old order Mennonite churches do not embrace musical instruments, they do celebrate God and the gift of Jesus through song. Sitting through a worship service and listening to the voices of the congregation lift up, in unison, to praise the birth of Jesus and glory of God is an experience that is not soon forgotten. The following are some of the favorite hymns and songs that I have heard sung at both Amish and Mennonite services.

GOOD CHRISTIAN MEN, REJOICE!

Good Christian men, rejoice
With heart, and soul, and voice,
Give ye heed to what we say!

News! News!
Jesus Christ is born to-day.
Ox and ass before Him bow,
And He is in the manger now.
Christ is born today!

Good Christian men, rejoice
With heart, and soul, and voice;
Now ye hear of endless bliss!

Joy! Joy!
Jesus Christ was born for this!
He hath opened the heavenly door,
And man is blessed evermore.
Christ was born for this!

Good Christian men, rejoice
With heart, and soul, and voice;
Now ye need not fear the grave :

Peace! Peace!
Jesus Christ was born to save,
Calls you one, and calls you all,
To gain His everlasting hall:
Christ was born to save.

J. M. Neale.

The Happy Morn

Christians, awake, salute the happy morn
Whereon the Savior of the world was born.
Rise to adore the mystery of love
Which hosts of angels chanted from above;
With them the joyful tidings first begun
Of God Incarnate and the Virgin's Son.

Then to the watchful shepherds it was told,
Who heard the angelic herald's voice,
"Behold, I bring good tidings of a Savior's birth
To you and all the nations upon earth:
This day hath God fulfilled His promised word,
This day is born a Savior, Christ the Lord."

He spake; and straightway the celestial choir
In hymns of joy, unknown before, conspire:
The praises of redeeming love they sang,
And Heaven's whole orb with Alleluias rang:
God's highest glory was their anthem still,
Peace upon earth, and unto men good will.

To Bethlehem straight the enlightened shepherds ran,

To see the wonder God had wrought for man,
And found, with Joseph and the blessed maid,
Her Son, the Savior, in a manger laid:
Then to their flocks, still praising God, return,
And their glad hearts with holy rapture burn.

O, may we keep and ponder in our mind

God's wondrous love in saving lost mankind;
Trace we the Babe, Who hath retrieved our loss,
From His poor manger to His bitter Cross;
Tread in His steps, assisted by His grace,
Till man s first heavenly state again takes place.

Then may we hope, the Angelic hosts among,
To sing, redeemed, a glad triumphal song:
He that was born upon this joyful day
Around us all His glory shall display:
Saved by His love, incessant we shall sing
Eternal praise to Heaven's Almighty King.

J. Byrom

THE HERALD ANGELS

Hark the herald angels sing
Glory to the new-born King,
Peace on earth, and mercy mild;
God and sinners reconciled!

Joyful all ye nations rise,
Join the triumph of the skies!
With the angelic host proclaim,
"Christ is born in Bethlehem!"
Hark! The herald angels sing
"Glory to the newborn King!

Christ by highest heaven adored,
Christ the everlasting Lord!
Late in time behold Him come
Offspring of a Virgin's womb
Veiled in flesh the Godhead see
Hail the incarnate Deity
Pleased as man with man to dwell
Jesus, our Emmanuel
Hark! The herald angels sing
"Glory to the newborn King!"

Hail the heaven-born Prince of Peace!
Hail the Son of Righteousness!
Light and life to all He brings
Ris'n with healing in His wings
Mild He lays His glory by
Born that man no more may die
Born to raise the sons of earth
Born to give them second birth

Hark! The herald angels sing
"Glory to the newborn King!"

Veiled in flesh the Godhead see,
Hail the incarnate Deity.

Hail the heaven-born Prince of Peace 1
Hail the Sun of Righteousness!
Light and life to all He brings,
Risen with healing in His wings.

Mild He lays His glory by,
Born that man no more may die;
Born to raise the sons of earth,
Born to give them second birth.

Come, Desire of Nations, come,
Fix in us Thy humble home;
Second Adam from above,
Reinstate us in Thy love.

C. Wesley.

THE FIRST NOËL

The first Noël the Angel did say,
Was to certain poor shepherds in fields as they lay-
In the fields where they lay, keeping their sheep,
On a cold winter's night that was freezing so deep.

Noël, Noël, Noël, Noël
Born is the King of Israel.

They looked up, and saw a star,
Shining in the East beyond them far
And to the earth it gave great light,
And so it continued both day and night.

Noël, Noël, Noël, Noël
Born is the King of Israel.

And by the light of that same star,
Three wise men came from country far;
To seek for a King was their intent,
And to follow the star wherever it went.

Noël, Noël, Noël, Noël
Born is the King of Israel.

This star drew nigh to the north-west,
O'er Bethlehem it took its rest;
And there did it both stop and stay,
Right over the place where Jesus lay.

Noël, Noël, Noël, Noël
Born is the King of Israel.

Then entered in those wise men three,
Fell reverently upon their knee;
And offered there, in His presence
Their gold, and myrrh, and frankincense.

Noël, Noël, Noël, Noël
Born is the King of Israel.

Then let us all with one accord,
Sing praises to our heavenly Lord;
That hath made Heaven and earth of nought,
And with His Blood mankind hath bought.

Noël, Noël, Noël, Noël
Born is the King of Israel.

Anon.

Silent Night

Silent night, holy night!
All is calm, all is bright.
Round yon Virgin, Mother and Child.
Holy infant so tender and mild,
Sleep in heavenly peace,
Sleep in heavenly peace

Silent night, holy night!
Shepherds quake at the sight.
Glories stream from heaven afar
Heavenly hosts sing Alleluia,
Christ the Savior is born!
Christ the Savior is born

Silent night, holy night!
Son of God love's pure light.
Radiant beams from Thy holy face
With dawn of redeeming grace,
Jesus Lord, at Thy birth
Jesus Lord, at Thy birth

My grandparents, Harlan and Sarah Marie Nice circa 1933 from the private collection of Sarah Price.

RECIPES

ESSENTIAL INGREDIENTS

Whether cooking for eight people or eighty people, both Amish and Mennonite cooks focus on organization, structure, and functionality in the kitchen. Good kitchen managers always keep these basic supplies in the pantry:

Baking powder
Butter
Cornstarch
Cream
Eggs (free range organic are preferred)
Flour
Milk (whole milk preferred)
Onions
Pepper
Potatoes
Salt
Shortening (or lard)
Sugar
Yeast

With just those ingredients, the following recipes can be made:

Baked Omelet
Basic Breads
German Potato Cakes
Pancakes
Potato Soup
Waffles

Obviously, with more ingredients, more recipes can be created. But as long as your kitchen stocks those basic ingredients, you have the foundation for a plain and simple meal.

OTHER ESSENTIAL ITEMS

As with the above, it's important to keep your pantry stocked with the following items. They come in handy for many recipes.

Applesauce

Carrots

Celery

Garlic

Ketchup

Maple Syrup

Molasses

Mustard

Oatmeal

Parsley

Pasta Noodles

Thyme

Please note that all recipes in this book serve 6-8 people unless otherwise stated.

BEVERAGES & PUNCH

At most meals, water and coffee are the beverage of choice. That does not mean, however, that at more festive gatherings, different drinks might be added to the menu. The following recipes are some that might be offered after an especially cold day or if family members gather to celebrate a birthday or special holiday.

BASIC PUNCH

Ingredients

- ½ cup sugar
- 1 cup water
- 1 can of frozen orange juice
- 1 can of frozen grapefruit juice
- 1 bottle of ginger ale (large)

Directions

1. Boil the water and put in the sugar.
2. Once dissolved, remove from the heat and cool.
3. Mix with the remaining ingredients to serve.

Variations (choose one):

1. Place some frozen sorbet in the punch bowl so that it slowly dissolves.
2. Swap cranberry juice with the grapefruit juice
3. Float small orange slices on top of the punch.
4. Mix different packages of flavored gelatin into the punch (for taste as well as coloring).

CRANBERRY PUNCH

Ingredients

- 1 package of cranberries (fresh or frozen)
- 2 cups of sugar
- 2 quarts of water
- 2-3 cinnamon sticks
- 1 can frozen orange juice
- 1 bottle of ginger ale (large)

Directions

1. Boil the water and cook the cranberries with the cinnamon sticks until cranberries are soft and mushy.
2. Drain the liquid and put it back in the pot.
3. Add the sugar and orange juice.
4. When ready to serve, add the ginger ale.

Decorating Tip

Put some of the cranberry skins into a small bowl of water and freeze. When ready to serve the punch, put the decorated ice into the punch bowl. Alternatively, put thin layers of oranges into the water for freezing.

EGG NOG

Ingredients

- 4 eggs
- 4 cups milk
- 2 cups cream
- ¾ cup sugar
- ½ teaspoon vanilla extract
- ½ teaspoon nutmeg
- 1 teaspoon ground cinnamon
- Grated nutmeg to garnish

Directions

1. In a large saucepan, combine the milk, nutmeg, cinnamon, and vanilla.
2. Cook on medium low heat until the mixture comes to a low boil, stirring occasionally.
3. In a separate bowl, combine the egg yolks and the sugar, and beat or whisk until fluffy.
4. Over low heat, combine both mixtures and stir frequently.
5. Refrigerate until ready to serve.
6. Garnish with grated nutmeg (or cinnamon sticks).

Momma Dee's Ski Tea

Contributed by Lisa Bull

This is great on the evening of December 25th, by a fire in the fireplace. Begin with steeping a large pot of hot tea. For each cup of Ski Tea, do the following:

1. Make a ¼ inch thick round cross-slice of fresh orange.
2. Poke three whole cloves into the orange slice.
3. Pour hot tea into a cup and stir in honey to taste.
4. Float the orange slice on the tea.
5. Stir with a cinnamon stick.

I serve this in my Currier and Ives cups and saucers, because they are short and squat, and so they are large enough in diameter to accommodate a slice of orange, and short enough to not swallow up the cinnamon stick.

Root Beer

Ingredients

- 2 cups white sugar
- 1 gallon lukewarm water
- 1 teaspoon yeast
- 4 teaspoons root beer extract

Directions

1. Use some warm water to dissolve yeast.
2. Add the sugar and root beer extract and mix thoroughly.
3. Put into a glass gallon jar.
4. Set in sun for 4 hours.
5. Ready to drink next day (after refrigeration).
6. Makes 1 gallon.

Note: Root beer extract can be purchased in most food stores in the spice aisle.

BREAKFAST TREATS

Breakfast is the time when family members gather together and plan their day. The good food served at this meal will nourish both body and soul. In today's world, many of us grab a quick bite to eat and run out the door, not pausing to spend time or sit around the table to enjoy a good meal. Take some time to try one of these hearty recipes with your family. You might find that your day shines a bit brighter, even on the coldest of mornings.

BAKED OMELET

Ingredients

- 8 eggs
- 1 cup milk
- ½ teaspoon seasoning salt
- 3 ounces cooked ham, diced
- ½ cup shredded Cheddar cheese
- ½ cup shredded mozzarella cheese
- ½ onion, minced

Directions

1. Preheat oven to 350 ° F.
2. Grease one 8x8 inch casserole dish and set aside.
3. Beat together the eggs and milk.
4. Add seasoning salt, ham, Cheddar cheese, Mozzarella cheese and minced onion.
5. Pour into prepared casserole dish.
6. Bake uncovered for 40 to 45 minutes.

Cheesy Breakfast Casserole

Ingredients

- 1 pound sliced bacon, diced
- 1 sweet onion, chopped
- 4 cups shredded potatoes (peeled, not cooked or frozen shredded hash brown potatoes, thawed)
- 9 eggs, lightly beaten
- 2 cups shredded Cheddar cheese
- 1 ½ cups small curd cottage cheese
- 1 ¼ cups shredded Swiss cheese

Directions

1. Preheat oven to 350 ° F.
2. Grease a 9x13-inch baking dish.
3. Heat a large skillet over medium-high heat; cook and stir bacon and onion until bacon is evenly browned, about 10 minutes.
4. Drain.
5. Transfer bacon and onion to a large bowl and stir in potatoes, eggs, Cheddar cheese, cottage cheese, and Swiss cheese.
6. Pour mixture into prepared baking dish.
7. Bake in preheated oven until eggs are set and cheese is melted, 45 to 50 minutes.
8. Let stand before cutting and serving.

Hash Browns

Ingredients

- 3 potatoes, peeled
- 1 onion, diced
- 3 tablespoons butter
- 1 pinch cayenne pepper, or to taste
- 1 pinch paprika, or to taste
- Salt and pepper to taste

Directions

1. Shred potatoes into a large bowl filled with cold water. Stir until water is cloudy, drain, and cover potatoes again with fresh cold water. Stir again to dissolve excess starch.
2. Drain potatoes well, pat dry with paper towels, and squeeze out any excess moisture.
3. Heat butter in a large non-stick pan over medium heat. Sprinkle shredded potatoes and onions into the hot butter and season with salt, black pepper, cayenne pepper, and paprika.
4. Cook potatoes until a brown crust forms on the bottom, about 5 minutes.
5. Continue to cook and stir until potatoes are browned all over, about 5 more minutes.

Baked Potato Cakes

Ingredients

- 2 onions, chopped
- 4 tablespoons butter
- 4 eggs
- 3 cups mashed potatoes
- 1/2 cup flour
- 2 tablespoon water
- Salt and pepper to taste

Directions

1. Preheat oven to 375° F.
2. In a large skillet, melt the butter.
3. Cook the onion until tender.
4. Remove from the heat.
5. In a large bowl, lightly beat two eggs.
6. Add the onion, potatoes, flour, salt, pepper and hot pepper sauce if desired.
7. Shape into four to six patties; place on a greased baking sheet.
8. Lightly beat remaining eggs.
9. Stir in water.
10. Brush over potato cakes.
11. Bake for 20-25 minutes or until heated through.

Waffles

Ingredients

- 2 eggs
- 2 cups all-purpose flour
- 1 3/4 cups milk
- 1/2 cup vegetable oil
- 1 tablespoon white sugar
- 4 teaspoons baking powder
- ¼ teaspoon salt
- 1/2 teaspoon vanilla extract

Directions

1. Preheat waffle iron.
2. Beat eggs in large bowl with hand beater until fluffy.
3. Beat in flour, milk, vegetable oil, sugar, baking powder, salt and vanilla.
4. Spray preheated waffle iron with non-stick cooking spray.
5. Pour mix onto hot waffle iron.
6. Cook until golden brown.
7. Serve hot.

BREADS

Once you start making home-made bread in your house, you will never want to stop. The sweet smell of bread baking in the oven seems to fill every nook and cranny of the home. When children return from school or grandchildren come to visit, welcome them with some fresh baked bread or muffins and watch their eyes light up when they walk into the kitchen.

In an Amish home, no meal is complete without bread. Whether served as rolls, sliced bread, or muffins, the table always has at least one, if not more, baskets with freshly baked bread to feed the family.

The following are some simple recipes to make bread and rolls. Additionally, a few more complicated recipes are included.

Basic Bread Recipe

Ingredients

- 5-6 cups flour
- 2 cups water (warm to the touch)
- 3 tablespoons sugar
- 1 tablespoon salt
- 2 tablespoons butter (or substitute with vegetable or corn oil)
- 1 package yeast

Directions

1. In a large bowl, dissolve the yeast in warm water. It will start to foam when it is dissolved.
2. Add the sugar, salt, butter and 3 cups flour. Beat until smooth. Stir in enough remaining flour to form a soft dough. If it gets sticky, add some more flour.
3. Knead until smooth and elastic, about 8-10 minutes.
4. Return the dough to the large bowl, greasing it lightly with oil (or more melted butter).
5. Cover and let it rise until doubled in size, usually about an hour or more. Avoid placing it in a drafty location.

6. Punch down the dough before removing it to place it on a lightly floured surface. Divide the dough into two equal pieces and shape each into a loaf.
7. Place each loaf into a greased 9-in. x 5-inch loaf pans. Cover and let them rise until doubled, about 30-45 minutes.
8. Brush the top with more oil or melted butter before baking at 375° F for 30-35 minutes or until golden brown and bread sounds hollow when tapped.
9. Remove from pans and place on wire racks to cool.

Basic Croissant Rolls

Ingredients

- 2 packages active dry yeast
- ¾ cup warm water
- ½ cup white sugar
- 1 teaspoon salt
- 2 eggs
- ½ cup butter, room temperature
- 4 cups all-purpose flour
- ¼ cup butter, softened

Directions

1. Dissolve yeast in warm water.
2. Stir in sugar, salt, eggs, butter, and 2 cups of flour.
3. Beat until smooth.
4. Mix in remaining flour until smooth.
5. Knead dough, then cover it and let rise in a warm place until double (about 1½ hours).
6. Punch down dough.
7. Divide in half.
8. Roll each half into a 12-inch circle.
9. Spread with butter.
10. Cut into 10 to 15 wedges.

11. Roll up the wedges starting with the wide end. You can also slightly bend the ends to give the croissants a crescent shape.

12. Place rolls with point under on a greased baking sheet. Cover and let rise until double (about 1 hour).

13. Bake at 400° F for 12-15 minute or until golden brown.

14. Brush tops with butter when they come out of the oven.

BASIC DINNER ROLLS

Ingredients

- Same as basic bread recipe

Directions

1. Use the same recipe for making basic bread.
2. Instead of rolling into two larger loaves, cut into small pieces and roll between your palms into balls.
3. Place two balls into each cup of a muffin pan.
4. Let rise until the tops are rounded and puffed just over the top of the muffin cup.
5. Preheat oven to 350° F.
6. Bake for 20 to 25 minutes, or until the tops are golden brown.

BLUEBERRY MUFFINS

Ingredients

- 1 cup milk
- ½ cup butter, melted
- 1 egg, slightly beaten
- 2 cups flour
- ⅓ cup sugar
- 1 tablespoon baking powder
- 1 teaspoon salt
- 1 cup fresh or frozen blueberries (thawed)

Topping: ¼ cup melted butter, ¼ cup sugar

Directions

1. Preheat oven to 400° F.
2. In large bowl, combine milk, butter and egg.
3. Add all remaining ingredients and mix.
4. Add the blueberries.
5. Spoon into greased 12-cup muffin pan.
6. Bake for 24-28 minutes or until golden brown.
7. Cool slightly; remove from pan.
8. Dip tops of muffins in a little melted butter, then in sugar.

Makes 1 dozen muffins.

Cinnamon Crescent Roll

Ingredients

- 1 package of ready-made crescent rolls OR make your own from the recipe in the bread section
- 2 tablespoons cinnamon
- 2 tablespoons sugar
- 2 tablespoons butter

Directions

1. Preheat oven to 350° F.
2. If making your own pastry, follow directions for making crescent pastry in previous section but, after rolling out and cutting into triangles, set them on a baking tray.
3. If using a ready-made pastry, separate into eight triangles.
4. Mix equal parts sugar and cinnamon in a bowl.
5. Melt butter.
6. Brush the pastry with melted butter.
7. Sprinkle on the crescent pastry (about half a teaspoon).
8. Roll the crescent rolls, long side to point.
9. Bake for 10 minutes.

Pumpkin Muffins

Ingredients:

- 1 ¾ cups all purpose flour
- 1 cup sugar
- ½ cup dark brown sugar
- 1 teaspoon baking soda
- ½ teaspoon salt
- 2 teaspoons cinnamon
- ¼ teaspoon ground cloves
- ¼ teaspoon nutmeg
- 2 eggs
- 1 can (15 ounces) pure pumpkin puree
- ½ cup shortening
- 1 teaspoon vanilla or almond extract.

Directions:

1. Preheat the oven to 375° F.
2. Line the wells of standard size muffin baking pan (or use liners).
3. Mix all of the dry ingredients in a medium sized bowl and set aside.
4. Mix the wet ingredients in another medium sized bowl.
5. Combine the wet and dry ingredients and stir.

6. Pour batter into the greased wells (or liners) until they are nearly full.
7. Bake for 20-22 minutes.

Makes 1 dozen muffins.

HINT: I use a gravy ladle in order to keep from dripping batter onto the tray.

Zucchini Bread

Ingredients

- 2-3 zucchini, grated (use a wide hole grater)
- 1 apple, grated
- 1 cup sugar
- ⅔ cup vegetable oil
- 2 teaspoons vanilla
- 4 eggs
- 3 cups flour
- 2 teaspoons baking soda
- 1 teaspoon salt
- 1 teaspoon ground cinnamon
- ½ teaspoon baking powder
- ½ cup nuts (pecan or walnuts, chopped)
- ½ cup raisins or dried cranberries, optional

Directions

1. Preheat oven to 350° F and grease bottoms only of a 9x5-inch loaf pan.
2. In large bowl, mix the zucchini and apple before adding sugar, oil, vanilla and eggs. Stir in remaining ingredients except nuts and raisins.

3. Optional: toast the nuts for a few minutes or salute the in some butter with a tablespoon of sugar.
4. Stir in nuts and raisins.
5. Pour batter into 9-inch pan.
6. Bake until toothpick inserted in center comes out clean (approximately 50 minutes)
7. Cool in pans on cooling rack 10 minutes.
8. Loosen sides of loaves from pans; remove from pans and place top side up on cooling rack.
9. Cool completely, about two hours, before slicing.

NOTE: Can be frozen.

STARTERS

In my experience with both Amish and Mennonite gatherings, I have not witnessed much emphasis on appetizers being served. Of course, they might have a bowl of chips and dip or pretzels, store-bought. However, I found these few goodies at post-church fellowship and family reunions.

APPLE AND CHEESE DIP

Ingredients

- Several apples, cored and cut into eighths
- 1 package of cream cheese (8 ounces)—soften before starting this recipe
- ¾ cup sugar, brown
- ¼ cup sugar, white
- 2 teaspoons vanilla or almond extract

Directions

1. Mix the room-temperature cream cheese with sugars and extract until smooth.
2. Place in a small bowl at the center of a plate.
3. Surround with cut apples for a nice before-meal treat.

CUP CHEESE

Ingredients
- 2 cups whole milk
- 2 pounds sharp cheese
- Salt and pepper to taste

Directions
1. Melt the cheese in a little bit of milk over medium heat.
2. Continue adding milk until it reaches the desired consistency.
3. Remove from heat and store in containers.
4. Best served with small, salted pretzels or on fresh baked bread.

NOTE: Experiment with different cheeses to see what flavors you like the best.

Deviled Eggs

Ingredients

- 6 eggs
- ¼ cup mayonnaise
- 1 teaspoon white vinegar
- 1 teaspoon yellow mustard
- ⅛ teaspoon salt
- Pepper to taste
- Paprika, for garnish

Directions

1. Place eggs in a single layer in a saucepan and cover with enough water so that a minimum of 1½ inches of water are above the eggs.
2. Heat on high until water begins to boil, then cover, turn the heat to low, and cook for 1 minute.
3. Remove from heat and leave covered for 14 minutes, then rinse under cold water continuously for 1 minute.
4. Crack egg shells and carefully peel under cool running water. Gently dry with paper towels.
5. Slice the eggs in half lengthwise, removing yolks to a medium bowl, and placing the whites on a serving platter.
6. Mash the yolks into a fine crumble using a fork.

7. Add mayonnaise, vinegar, mustard, salt, and pepper, and mix well.

8. Evenly disperse the yolk mixture into the egg whites.

9. Sprinkle with paprika and serve.

NOTE: For a special "bling", cut the eggs at the top so that they stand up (vs. halving them) and decorate the plate with parsley.

Ham Balls

Ingredients

- 1 ½ pounds ground pork
- 1 ½ pounds ground beef
- 2 eggs
- 2 cups bread crumbs
- 1 cup milk
- 1 ½ cups sugar, brown
- ½ cup vinegar
- ½ cup water
- 1 tablespoon mustard

Directions

1. Preheat oven to 350 ° F.
2. Mix together the ham, beef, and bread crumbs.
3. In a small bowl, beat the eggs.
4. Add the milk and mix.
5. Combine with the meat.
6. Add salt and pepper to taste.
7. Roll into small balls (about 20-26).
8. Place in a baking dish.
9. For the sauce, combine the sugar, mustard, vinegar, and water and pour over the ham balls.

10. Bake for two hours.
11. May be frozen.

NOTE: Serve with festive colored toothpicks. May also be served as a side for the meal.

Micheline Salad

Contributed by Marc J. Schumacher

Ingredients

- 2 cans of diced beets, or sliced.
- 4 cans of sweet kernel corn
- ¼ cup mayonnaise
- ⅛ teaspoon salt
- Pepper to taste
- Paprika and/or parsley for garnish

Directions

1. Drain the beets in a strainer and wash them under cold water until the water runs almost clear. If you are using sliced beets just cut them into small pieces.
2. Drain the liquid from the corn.
3. In a large glass bowl, mix the beets and the corn as well as ¾ of the mayonnaise and add pepper and salt to taste.
4. Smooth level the top of the mixture in the bowl and add the rest of the mayonnaise as a thin layer.
5. Garnish with a little paprika or parsley or both.

6. (Optional) If you feel adventurous, you can add a few tablespoons of mint jelly to the mixture.
7. Refrigerate before serving.

SOUPS

When you work hard, you get hungry. When you combine work with the cold weather, soup is always a welcomed treat. Personally, during the winter months, I could live on soup. These soups tend to be served during the supper hour on cold nights, when both Amish and Mennonite families tend to have a lighter meal.

Serve with warm bread or rolls for an extra cheer from your family.

Basic Amish Soup

Ingredients

- 4 slices bread
- 2 tablespoons butter
- 1 cup water
- ½ cup cream
- Salt and pepper to taste

Directions

1. Cut the slices of bread into small squares (optional, roll into small balls)
2. In a small pot, melt the butter.
3. Add the bread cubes (or balls).
4. When browned, remove from heat and put into bowls.
5. In same sauce pan, add water, cream, and salt.
6. Stirring constantly, heat the liquids. Do not boil.
7. When hot, pour into the bowls with the bread and serve.

Chicken Corn Soup

Contributed by Eleanor H. Nice

Ingredients

- 1 chicken (approximately 4 pounds)
- ½ cup chopped celery and leaves
- 4 quarts of cold water
- 10 ears of corn
- 1 onion, chopped
- 2 cooked eggs
- Salt and pepper to taste
- Parsley, chopped (optional)

Directions

1. Cook chicken slowly until it is tender. Add salt about 30 minutes before it is finished.
2. Remove the chicken and strain the broth.
3. Return broth to pan.
4. Remove the meat from the chicken.
5. Chop it fine and return to broth.
6. Remove the corn from the cob and put into broth along with the chopped celery and desired amount of salt and pepper.

7. Ten minutes before serving, drop in chopped egg and parsley and small dumplings made from:
    1. 1 cup of flour
    2. ¼ cup milk
    3. 1 egg
8. Rub or blend this mixture together with two forks until well mixed and drop into boiling soup.
9. Cover and cook for 7 minutes.

NOTE: Can be made in advance and/or frozen.

Chicken Noodle Soup

Ingredients

- 4 pounds chicken
- 2½ quarts water
- 2½ teaspoons salt
- 3 cups cooked noodles
- 1 carrot, sliced
- 1 celery, diced
- 1 bay leaf
- Salt and pepper to taste
- Parsley for garnish

Directions

1. Cut a young stewing chicken into serving pieces, add to a pot of salted water, bring to a boil and simmer for 2½ hours, adding additional water as needed.
2. Skim off the fat and add the onion, carrot, celery, bay leaf, salt and pepper.
3. Bring to boil again before adding the noodles.
4. Cook for 20 minutes longer

Cream of Mushroom Soup

Ingredients

- 1 ½ pounds mushrooms, thinly sliced
- 4 cups chicken broth
- 1 cup cream
- ¼ cup unsalted butter
- 3 cloves garlic, minced
- 1 onion, diced
- ½ teaspoon dried thyme
- 2 tablespoons cornstarch
- Salt and pepper, to taste

Directions

1. Melt butter over medium heat.
2. Add garlic and mushrooms, and cook, stirring occasionally, until tender and browned.
3. Stir in onion and cook, stirring frequently, until translucent, about 2-3 minutes.
4. Reduce heat and simmer until slightly reduced, about 5 minutes. Stir in chicken broth, heavy cream and thyme.
5. In a small bowl, whisk together cornstarch and ¼ cup water.
6. Stir in mixture to the soup until slightly thickened, about 1-2 minutes;

7. Add more cornstarch as needed until desired consistency is reached.
8. Add salt and pepper, to taste.

NOTE: Substitute celery or chicken for mushrooms if desired or needed for recipes.

Oyster Stew

Ingredients

- 2 cans small to medium-sized raw shucked oysters (can be fresh but keep the liquid)
- 3 cups milk (or use 1 quart of half and half)
- 4 tablespoons butter
- 2 tablespoons shallot (or onion), finely chopped
- 1 or 2 dashes hot sauce (or use cayenne pepper)
- Minced parsley, sliced chives, or sliced green onions (your choice)
- Salt and pepper to taste

Directions

1. The most important factors in preparing Oyster Stew are to not boil the milk and to not overcook the oysters. Be careful to avoid overcooking oysters, as it causes them to become tough.
2. Drain the oysters, reserving their liquor.
3. In a large pan over medium heat, melt butter.
4. Add the shallots (or onions) and cook until transparent.
5. Add the oysters and simmer very gently for about 2 to 4 minutes.
6. While the oysters are simmering, in a separate saucepan over low heat, slowly heat the milk, cream, and oyster liquor (do not boil).

7. When the oysters are cooked, slowly add the hot milk mixture to the oysters, stirring gently. Do not scald or burn the milk.
8. Season with hot sauce (or cayenne pepper).
9. Add salt and pepper to taste.
10. Remove from heat to serve.

NOTE: Garnish each bowl with parsley, chives, or green onions.

Potato Soup

Ingredients

- ⅔ cup flour (less if thicker consistency desired)
- 7-8 cups milk
- 4 large potatoes
- 1 medium onion
- 12 bacon strips, cooked & crumbled
- 1¼ cups shredded cheddar cheese
- Salt and Pepper to taste
- Parsley for garnish

Directions

1. Peel and dice the potato and onions.
2. Boil potatoes and onion in small amount of water until soft.
3. Add milk, salt and pepper then reheat.
4. Brown flour in the butter and blend it slowly into the potato mixture.
5. Add a little water to the beaten egg and stir into the soup.
6. Let it cook for a few minutes and serve with a sprinkling of chopped parsley.

MAIN DISHES

For every Amish and Mennonite family, hearty food is a must, especially in the colder months. These recipes are tried-and-true classics. With simple ingredients and easy instructions, even the most timid of cooks will shine like bright stars and warm their families' kitchen table!

BACON, LETTUCE, TOMATO SANDWICH

Contributed by Stanley A. Nice

This recipe doesn't really need ingredients or instructions. But it does deserve to be explained. When I was growing up, my father sold poultry. This was back in the 1940s. He would work at market in different cities during the week. It was long days and hours to manage the poultry and sell them to his customers.

By the time Saturday came around, he was tired and ready to relax with the family. He only worked half a day on Saturdays so Mother would make a large dinner for the noon meal. The next day, we would rise early and attend church. In the afternoons, we would visit with family—we had plenty of relatives that lived nearby! So, on Saturday evenings, Mother would always serve us these sandwiches with store-bought chips and refrigerator pickles.

It was easy to make and even easier to clean up so that she was not stuck in the kitchen. She, too, wanted to enjoy time with her family.

Ingredients

- Bacon
- Lettuce

- Tomato, sliced
- Fresh bread, sliced
- Cheddar cheese
- Mayonnaise

Directions

1. Spread mayonnaise on both sides of the bread.
2. Layer the bacon, tomato, and lettuce (not shredded).
3. Put some cheddar cheese on top of the other ingredients.
4. Close the sandwich.
5. Serve with chips and pickles.

BAKED HAM

Ingredients

- 6 pound ham (preference is spiral cut with bone-in)
- 1 cup milk
- 8 tablespoons sugar, brown
- 3 tablespoons mustard
- 2 tablespoons cider vinegar

Directions

1. Preheat oven to 350 ° F.
2. Mix the milk, sugar, mustard, and vinegar.
3. Place the ham in a roasting pan.
4. Spread the dressing over the ham.
5. Cook 15 minutes for each pound (approximately 1 ½ hours for a 6 pound ham).

Chicken Pot Pie

Ingredients

- 1 chicken (cut into pieces)
- 4 potatoes, cubed
- 1 ½ cups flour
- 2 eggs
- 3 tablespoons cream
- 2 carrots, chopped
- 2 celery stalks, chopped
- Salt and pepper to taste

Directions

1. Preheat oven to 350 ° F.
2. Cook pieces of chicken in water.
3. When cooked, remove the chicken and season the water with salt and pepper. Alternatively, use chicken broth.
4. Cook the potatoes, carrots, and celery in the broth.
5. Place the chicken into a casserole dish.
6. Add the vegetables.
7. Pour some broth over the mixture (not covering).
8. In a small bowl, mix the eggs and cream together.

9. Add to a separate bowl containing the flour.
10. Mix until it turns into a soft dough.
11. Roll the dough and spread on top of the casserole.
12. Bake 30 minutes or until top crust is brown.

Chicken, Roasted

Ingredients

- 1 chicken (approximately 5 pounds)
- 2 tablespoon melted butter (or olive oil)
- 1 onion, thinly sliced
- 1 medium lemon, thinly sliced (optional)
- Fresh herbs, such as parsley, rosemary, or thyme (optional)
- Salt and pepper to taste

Directions

1. Preheat the oven to 425 ° F.
2. Remove giblets and neck from the chicken and rinse the inside cavity.
3. Pat dry with a paper towel.
4. Sprinkle salt and pepper inside the cavity.
5. Put onion and lemon inside the cavity with any herbs.
6. Place in a roasting pan.
7. Rub butter (or oil) on the outside of the chicken and add some salt and pepper.
8. Roast for approximately 1 hour or until the juices run clear.

Ham Loaf

Ingredients

- ½ lb. ground beef
- 1 lb. ground pork
- ½ cup bread crumbs
- 3 eggs
- 1 cup tomato juice (or tomato sauce)
- Ketchup (optional)

Directions

1. Boil water and cook one of the eggs. Let cool before removing the shell.
2. Preheat oven to 350° F.
3. Combine all of the ingredients, except the ketchup.
4. Shape half of the meat mixture into a slightly greased loaf pan.
5. Place the hardboiled egg in the center. You might need to scoop out a little of the meat to make an indent for the egg.
6. Press the rest of the meat around the egg and fill the loaf pan.

ROASTED TURKEY

Ingredients

- 1 turkey (approximately 10 pounds)
- 1 onion
- 1 head of garlic
- Melted butter (or olive oil)
- Fresh herbs (thyme, rosemary, and/or parsley)
- Salt and pepper to taste

Directions

1. Preheat oven to 350 ° F.
2. Remove turkey parts from neck and breast cavities.
3. Rinse the cavity of the turkey and pat dry with paper towels.
4. Salt and pepper inside the breast cavity and stuff the onion, garlic, and herbs.
5. Place the turkey, breast side up, in a roasting pan.
6. Brush generously with the butter (or oil) and season with salt and pepper.
7. Cover the turkey with foil and roast for three hours.
8. Remove turkey from the oven and set aside to rest for 20 minutes before carving.

Lasagna

Ingredients

- 1 pound ground beef
- 4 cups tomato or pasta sauce
- 6 uncooked lasagna noodles
- 1 container ricotta cheese (15 ounces)
- 2 1/2 cups shredded mozzarella cheese
- 1 teaspoon oregano
- ¼ cup hot water

Directions

1. Preheat oven to 375° F.
2. In a large skillet over medium heat, cook the beef.
3. Drain.
4. Stir in tomato sauce with the meat.
5. In a separate bowl, mix the ricotta and mozzarella cheeses together.
6. Spread one-third of meat sauce in a lightly greased 11 x 7-inch baking dish;
7. Layer with three uncooked noodles and a thin layer of cheese mixture.
8. Repeat procedure.
9. Slowly pour ¼ cup hot water around inside edge of dish.

10. Tightly cover baking dish with 2 layers of heavy-duty aluminum foil.

11. Bake for 45 minutes; uncover and bake 10 more minutes.

12. Let stand 10 minutes before serving.

NOTE: Can be frozen.

MEATBALLS

Ingredients:

- 1 lb. ground beef
- ½ cup bread crumbs
- ½ cup carrots, shredded
- 1/4 cup onion
- 2 eggs
- ½ cup Parmesan cheese
- 1 teaspoon parsley
- ½ teaspoon garlic salt
- Salt and pepper

Directions:

1. Preheat oven to 350° F.
2. Combine all ingredients, mixing well.
3. Shape into meatballs, and either fry in oil or bake for 20-25 minutes until done.
4. Drain.
5. In some Amish homes, these might be served over mashed potatoes, rice, or pasta.

MEATLOAF SURPRISE

Ingredients

- 1 lb. ground beef
- ½ cup bread crumbs
- ½ cup carrots, shredded
- 1/4 cup onion, chopped into small pieces
- 3 eggs
- ½ cup Parmesan cheese
- 1 teaspoon parsley
- Ketchup
- Salt and pepper

Directions

1. Boil water and cook one of the eggs. Let cool before removing the shell.
2. Preheat oven to 350° F.
3. Combine all of the ingredients, except the ketchup.
4. Shape half of the meat mixture a slightly greased loaf pan.
5. Place the hardboiled egg in the center. You might need to scoop out a little of the meat to make an indent for the egg.
6. Press the rest of the meat around the egg and fill the loaf pan.

7. With a knife, cut a small slit along the top of the loaf and pour some ketchup in it.
8. Bake for 50-55 minutes until done.

NOTE: In some Amish homes, these might be served over mashed potatoes, rice, or pasta, with or without a sauce.

SAUSAGE AND SAUERKRAUT

Ingredients

- Sausage links
- Sauerkraut
- Capers, optional

Directions

1. Cook pork links in pot of salted water.
2. Add sauerkraut and simmer for three hours.
3. Optional: Add capers.

NOTE: Mix different types of sausage: pork, venison, beef, duck, etc.

SHEPHERD'S PIE

This is great for leftovers and makes for a wonderful fall and winter supper.

1. Preheat oven to 350° F.
2. Line a greased casserole with mashed potatoes.
3. Can be leftover potatoes or even store-bought ready-made mashed potatoes.
4. Fill the casserole now with leftover vegetables and meat cubes (or cooked ground hamburger, turkey, sausage, or ham).
5. Add bread crumbs to lightly cover and add leftover gravy or a tomato sauce.
6. Cover with mashed potatoes.
7. Bake for 40 minutes.

Workday Dinner

Ingredients

- 1 tablespoon butter
- 1 large yellow onion
- 5 large potatoes
- 2 tablespoons flour
- 1 can of tomato sauce (16 ounces)
- 1 pound of sausage (about 5 links)
- Salt and pepper to taste

Directions

1. Preheat oven to 350° F.
2. Slice the onion, potatoes and sausage
3. Melt the butter and pour into the bottom of a 9x13 casserole pan
4. Layer the onions and potatoes
5. Sprinkle the flour on top of the potatoes.
6. Evenly pour the tomato sauce over the potatoes.
7. Layer the sausage on top of the tomato sauce.
8. Add water to cover.
9. Bake for three hours.

SIDE DISHES: VEGETABLES & OTHERS

In the colder months, both Amish and Mennonite women tend to rely on canned or frozen vegetables to nourish their families. If you don't have access to a supply of fresh vegetables from the store, it's a good idea to stock up on frozen vegetables.

In our garage, I have a freezer just for meats and vegetables. It comes in handy during the winter months.

APPLESAUCE

Ingredients:

- 4-5 pounds of apples
- 1-2 cups of water
- 1 cup sugar
- Optional: 1 teaspoon of cinnamon
- Optional: 1 teaspoon of nutmeg

Directions:

1. Peel, core, and quarter the apples.
2. Place apples in a large saucepan and just barely cover with water.
3. Simmer over medium-low heat until apples are tender (approximately 15 minutes).
4. Using a hand masher, break up the apples until smooth (or run cooked apples through a food mill or blender).
5. Stir in the sugar to taste.
6. Cook over medium heat for about 3 to 5 minutes.
7. Serve warm or cool in the refrigerator. May also be frozen.

Baked Corn

Ingredients

- 2 cups cooked or canned corn (kernels)
- 2 tablespoons of unsalted butter
- 1 ½ tablespoons of flour
- 1 cup milk
- 1 tablespoon of sugar
- 2 eggs
- ½ cup buttered crumbs
- Salt and pepper to taste

Directions

1. Preheat oven to 350 ° F.
2. Melt the butter and add the flour.
3. Add milk and gradually bring to boiling point, stirring constantly to prevent sticking.
4. Add corn, salt and pepper and sugar and heat thoroughly.
5. Remove from heat and add the beaten eggs.
6. Pour into a greased baking dish and sprinkle the buttered crumbs on the top.
7. Bake for 25 minutes.

CARROT CASSEROLE

Ingredients

- 6-8 carrots (large)
- 1 onion, diced
- 2 celery stalks
- 4 slices of bread, cubed
- 2 eggs
- 3 tablespoons butter
- 1 teaspoon parsley
- Salt to taste

Directions

1. Preheat the oven to 350 ° F.
2. Peel carrots and dice into small bite-sized pieces.
3. Bring a pot of salted water to a boil and cook the carrots for 7-8 minutes (until tender).
4. Drain water from carrots.
5. Using a hand masher, mash the carrots.
6. In a saucepan, melt butter over a medium heat and cook the celery with the onions until translucent.
7. Add the eggs, parsley, and mashed carrots before pouring into a casserole dish.
8. Bake for 30 minutes.

Green Bean Casserole

Ingredients

- 1 can of cream of mushroom soup*
- ½ cup milk
- 1 teaspoon soy sauce
- 1 dash black pepper
- 4 cups green beans
- 1 ⅓ cups fried onions (may be store bought)

Directions

1. Preheat oven to 350° F.
2. Stir the soup, milk, soy sauce, black pepper, beans and ⅔ cup onions in a casserole dish.
3. Bake for 25 minutes or until the bean mixture is hot and bubbling.
4. Stir the bean mixture.
5. Sprinkle with more onions.
6. Bake for an additional 5 minutes or until the onions are golden brown.

*If you want to make cream of mushroom soup instead of using canned, see the recipe under SOUPS.

Maple Syrup Carrots

Ingredients

- 2 pounds carrots, sliced (or store-bought carrots)
- ¼ cup maple syrup
- ⅓ cup water
- 2 tablespoons unsalted butter
- Salt and pepper to taste

Directions

1. Combine the carrots, syrup, butter, and water in a pot over medium heat.
2. Bring to a boil.
3. Reduce heat and simmer until the carrots are tender and the liquid is reduced (about 15 minutes).
4. Add salt and pepper to taste.

Mashed Turnips

Ingredients

- 2 pounds turnips
- 6 tablespoons butter
- 2 teaspoons sugar
- Salt and pepper to taste.

Directions

1. Peel turnips and dice.
2. In a large pot of boiling water, add turnips and cook approximately 30 minutes.
3. Drain water.
4. Add butter and sugar.
5. Add salt and pepper to taste.
6. Using a hand masher, mash the turnips with butter and seasonings until reaching a desired consistency.

Sweet and Sour Green Beans

Contributed by Eleanor H. Nice

Ingredients

- 3 cups red wine vinegar
- 6 tablespoons of sugar
- 6 tablespoons (¾) stick of unsalted butter
- 3 pounds of green beans (trimmed)
- ⅓ cup of fresh parsley (chopped)

Directions

1. Boil red wine vinegar and sugar in heavy medium saucepan over medium-high heat until reduced to ¾ cups (approximately 45 minutes).
2. Add butter and whisk until melted.
3. Cover and refrigerate.
4. Cook beans in large pot of boiling salted water until just tender. Stir occasionally for about 8 minutes and then drain the water.
5. Pour vinegar mixture into same pot with drained beans and bring to simmer.
6. Toss to coat.
7. Season to taste with salt and pepper.
8. Mound beans in bowl and sprinkle with parsley and serve.

SIDE DISHES: STARCHES

Since the main meal is typically served at noon, both Amish and Mennonite women tend to serve heaping sides of starches. It's no wonder that there are plenty of recipes for potatoes, casseroles, and pasta dishes. Not only do the starches give the family energy for the afternoon and evening chores, it also warms them up on cold winter afternoons.

Amish Casserole

Ingredients

- 1 pound ground beef
- ¼ cup brown sugar
- ⅛ teaspoon black pepper
- ¼ teaspoon salt
- 1 can condensed tomato soup
- 1 can condensed cream of chicken soup
- 1 (12 ounce) package wide egg noodles
- 10 slices American cheese

Directions

1. Preheat the oven to 350° F.
2. Bring a large pot of lightly salted water to a boil.
3. Add egg noodles and cook until tender, about 7 minutes.
4. Drain and return to the pot.
5. Mix in the cream of chicken soup until noodles are coated.
6. Crumble the ground beef into a large skillet over medium-high heat.
7. Drain the grease, and stir in the tomato soup, brown sugar, pepper and salt.

8. Spread half of the beef in the bottom of a greased 2½ quart casserole dish.
9. Arrange 5 slices of cheese over the beef.
10. Top with half of the noodles, then repeat layers ending with cheese on top.
11. Bake for 35 minutes in the preheated oven, until cheese is browned and sauce is bubbly.

Baked Macaroni and Cheese

Ingredients

- ½ pound elbow macaroni
- 3 tablespoons butter
- 3 tablespoons flour
- 1 tablespoon powdered mustard
- 3 cups milk
- ½ cup yellow onion, finely diced
- 1 bay leaf
- ½ teaspoon paprika
- 1 large egg
- 12 ounces sharp cheddar, shredded
- 1 teaspoon kosher salt
- Fresh black pepper

Topping:

- 3 tablespoons butter
- 1 cup bread crumbs

Directions

1. Preheat oven to 350° F.
2. In a large pot, boil water and then cook the pasta to al dente.
3. In a separate pot, melt the butter.
4. Whisk in the flour and mustard for about five minutes.

5. Stir in the milk, onion, bay leaf, and paprika.
6. Simmer for ten minutes and remove the bay leaf.
7. Temper in the egg.
8. Stir in ¾ of the cheese.
9. Season with salt and pepper.
10. Fold the macaroni into the mix and pour into a 2-quart casserole dish.
11. Top with remaining cheese.
12. For the topping, melt the butter in a sauté pan and toss the bread crumbs to coat.
13. Top the macaroni with the bread crumbs.
14. Bake for 30 minutes.

Broccoli Casserole

Ingredients

- 1 can cream of mushroom soup
- 1 cup mayonnaise
- ½ cup chopped onion
- ½ teaspoon salt
- ¼ teaspoon black pepper
- 2 packages frozen chopped broccoli (20 ounces), thawed
- 1 cup shredded sharp Cheddar cheese
- 1 (6-ounce) box herbed stuffing mix
- ¼ cup (½ stick) butter, melted and divided

Directions

1. Preheat oven to 350 ° F.
2. Coat a 3-quart casserole dish with cooking spray.
3. In a medium bowl, combine soup, mayonnaise, onion, salt, and pepper; mix well.
4. Place half the broccoli in the casserole dish. Sprinkle with half the cheese and half the stuffing mix.
5. Pour half the butter and half the soup mixture over stuffing. Repeat layers one more time.

6. Bake 35 to 40 minutes, or until hot in center.

Candied Sweet Potatoes

Ingredients

- 6 large sweet potatoes
- 1/2 cup butter
- 2 cups sugar, white
- 1 teaspoon cinnamon
- 1 teaspoon nutmeg
- 1 tablespoon vanilla extract
- Salt to taste

- *Directions*

    1. Peel the sweet potatoes and cut them into ¼ inch slices.
    2. Melt the butter in a heavy skillet and add the potatoes.
    3. Mix the sugar, cinnamon, nutmeg and salt.
    4. Cover the sweet potatoes with sugar mixture and stir.
    5. Reduce heat to low and cook for about 1 hour or until potatoes are "candied."
    6. Stir in the vanilla.
    7. Serve hot.

Pennsylvania Dutch Corn Pie

Ingredients

- 1 large potato, peeled and chopped
- 1 can whole kernel corn, drained
- 1 can cream-style corn
- 3 hard-boiled eggs, chopped
- ½ cup milk
- 1 tablespoon butter
- Salt and pepper to taste
- Pie shell (see Pastries and Pies)

Directions

1. Preheat the oven to 425° F.
2. In a saucepan over medium heat, stir together the potato, whole kernel corn, creamed corn, hard boiled eggs, salt, pepper and milk.
3. Simmer for about 15 minutes.
4. Press one of the pie crusts into the bottom and up the sides of a 9-inch pie plate.
5. Pour the hot filling into the crust. Dot with pieces of butter.
6. Cover with the top crust, and flute the edges to seal.

7. Cut a few slits in the top crust to vent steam.
8. Place on a cookie sheet.
9. Bake for 30 minutes in the preheated oven, and then reduce the temperature to 350° F.
10. Bake for an additional 10 minutes, or until the crust is browned.
11. Serve hot.

Lisa's Sweet Potato Casserole

Contributed by Lisa Bull

Ingredients

- 3-4 cups cooked sweet potatoes
- ½ cup sugar
- ½ cup butter
- 2 eggs
- 1 teaspoon vanilla
- ⅓ cup sweet milk

Topping

- 1 cup light brown sugar
- ½ cup flour
- ⅓ cup butter (softened)
- 1 cup chopped pecans

Directions

1. Preheat oven to 350° F
2. Remove skins from the potatoes and mash them in a large bowl.
3. Mix in sugar and ½ cup butter.
4. In a smaller bowl, beat eggs, vanilla and sweet milk.
5. Mix with sweet potatoes.

6. Pour into baking dish.
7. Mix brown sugar, flour, ⅓ cup butter and pecans.
8. Sprinkle over sweet potatoes.
9. Bake for 25 minutes.

Mother-In-Law's Rice Casserole

Contributed by Lisa Bull

My mother-in-law taught me to make this way back when I was in high school. It is terrific for a quick meal. My boys also like it when they aren't feeling well. It's total comfort food for them. Serve with corn muffins and honey and a side of peas.

Ingredients

- 2 boil-in-bag white rice
- 2 boil-in-bag brown rice
- 2-3 cans cream of chicken soup
- 1 cup cheddar cheese
- A "little" milk
- 1 pound lean ground beef cooked and drained

Directions

1. Boil the rice and empty into large pot. Mix in all the other ingredients.
2. Serve in deep bowls.

Mashed Potatoes

Ingredients

- 1 ½ pounds potatoes
- 1/2 teaspoon salt
- 4 tablespoon heavy cream
- 2 tablespoon butter
- 1-2 tablespoons milk
- Salt and Pepper

Directions

1. Peel and cut potatoes into quarters.
2. Place the potatoes into a pot and cover with cold water.
3. Add a half teaspoon of salt to the water.
4. Bring the water to a boil.
5. Reduce the heat and simmer for 15 to 20 minutes.
6. In a separate saucepan, melt the butter and warm the cream.
7. Drain the liquid from the potatoes.
8. Pour the cream and melted butter over the potatoes.
9. Mash the potatoes with a hand masher.
10. Add milk and beat until the mashed potatoes are smooth.

11. Add salt and pepper to taste.

NOTE: Experiment by adding different herbs (rosemary, thyme, parsley) and/or garlic to the potatoes.

Oyster Stuffing

Contributed by Eleanor H. Nice

Ingredients

- 8 cups Trenton oyster crackers
- 5 containers of oysters (8 ounces each)
- Parsley to taste
- 8 eggs
- ½ lb. of butter
- 2 cups of chicken broth
- 5 cups of milk
- Salt and pepper to taste

Directions

1. Preheat oven to 350° F.
2. Crackers are to be broken into small pieces. Can wrap same in a kitchen towel and smash up with a rolling pin or meat tenderizer hammer.
3. Place cracker pieces in a large mixing bowl.
4. Cut the oysters in half.
5. Mix in with crackers. Include any juice in the containers from the oysters.
6. Add minced parsley to taste.
7. Beat eggs in a separate bowl and then add to crackers.

8. Melt butter and add along with the broth and the milk.
9. Add salt and pepper to taste.
10. When crackers and ingredients are all mixed, place in a greased baking dish.
11. Bake for 1½ hours. Can stir once or twice during baking. Add juices from any baked poultry or milk if the mixture seems to be drying out.

ROASTED BUTTERNUT SQUASH

Ingredients

- 2 large butternut squash
- 3 tablespoons butter (or olive oil)
- Salt
- Minced garlic (optional)

Directions

1. Preheat oven to 400° F.
2. Cut the squash lengthwise and remove the seeds.
3. Remove the rind of the squash (peeler or sharp coring knife works best).
4. Cut into one-inch cubes.
5. Put into a large bowl and drizzle melted butter or olive oil on top. Mix.
6. Sprinkle with salt and mix again.
7. Put onto a baking sheet and bake for approximately 25 minutes.

PICKLED DISHES & RELISHES

No Amish table would be complete without some dish that contains pickled vegetables or a relish. Believe it or not, they are very easy to make. Since they can be kept for a long time in the refrigerator, making a larger batch is as simple as doubling the ingredients.

Think green and keep the glass jars from spaghetti sauce to store these recipes in the pantry or refrigerator until you are ready to use them.

Amish Chow Chow

Ingredients

- 2 cups green beans
- 2 cups yellow beans
- 2 cups corn
- 2 cups cucumbers (cut into small pieces)
- 2 cups carrots (cut into small pieces)
- 2 cups lima beans (optional)
- 1 head of cabbage
- 4 stalks celery
- ½ dozen green tomatoes
- Large white onion
- 3 quarts vinegar
- 5 cups sugar
- 1 tablespoon celery seed
- Salt to taste.

Directions

1. Cook the first four ingredients (vegetables) until they are tender.
2. Drain them.
3. Chop all ingredients (including the tomatoes and onions) into small bite sizes.
4. Drain again.
5. Add salt.

6. Mix all ingredients together in a boiling syrup of vinegar, sugar, and celery seed.
7. Heat, jar, and seal.

NOTE: If you don't want to can it, at least let it sit for a few days. It will taste better.

CANNING: To properly can the chow-chow, bring water to a boil. Pack hot relish into hot jars, leaving ½-inch headspace. Remove air bubbles. Adjust two-piece caps. Process pints 10 minutes in a boiling-water canner.

PICKLED BEETS

Ingredients

- 8 to 10 beets
- 4 cups vinegar
- 1 cup water (plus water to boil beets)
- 2 cups sugar
- ½ teaspoon pickling spice
- Salt and pepper to taste

Directions

1. Bring a pot of salted water to a boil.
2. Trim tops of the beets, leaving some of the top.
3. Cook the beets until tender.
4. Drain and cool with cold water.
5. Remove the tops and bottoms before slipping off the outer skin.
6. Cut beets into smaller pieces.
7. In a sauce pan, combine remaining ingredients and bring to a boil.
8. Add beets and boil for ten minutes.
9. Pour into jars, cover, and refrigerate.

Pickled Cabbage

Contributed by Stanley A. Nice

Ingredients
- 1 head of cabbage
- 1 red pepper
- 1 green pepper
- Salt
- Sugar
- White vinegar
- 1 head of cabbage
- 3 celery stalks

Directions
1. This is best if done at least a day ahead as it lets the favor address the cabbage; however, if time does not permit, do not worry.
2. Using a food processor or hand shredder, shred the head of cabbage and the celery. Place the shredded vegetables in a large mixing bowl.
3. Add a small amount of red pepper and green pepper after it is chopped by the food processor.
4. Usually about ½ pepper will be enough. More if you like peppers; less if they aren't your favorite. The peppers do add great color

to the cabbage so even a little is better than none.

5. Sprinkle with sugar and mix the cabbage and peppers together.
6. Add about 1 cup of white vinegar. Stir and taste. If too sour, add some sugar; if too sweet, add more vinegar.

NOTE: This was always a favorite addition to our holiday dinners. Mom-Mom made this so often that it was not possible to get accurate measurements from her. You will find that it isn't difficult to make and you can adjust the favor to whatever you prefer. Enjoy.

PICKLED EGGS

Ingredients

- 2 cups vinegar
- 1 cup water
- ½ cup sugar
- 6-8 eggs, hard boiled
- Salt and pepper to taste

Directions

1. In a sauce pan, bring water and vinegar to a boil.
2. Add sugar and stir until dissolved.
3. Remove from heat and let cool
4. Put shelled hard boiled eggs into two jars.
5. Add liquid.
6. Put a pinch of salt and pepper into each jar.
7. Cover and refrigerate.

REFRIGERATOR PICKLES

Ingredients

- 2 pounds of cucumbers
- 2 onions
- 3 tablespoons salt
- 2 cups vinegar
- 4 cups sugar
- 1 teaspoon celery seed
- 1 teaspoon turmeric
- Salt and pepper to taste

Directions

1. Mix the cucumbers, onions, and salt.
2. Let sit for three hours or longer.
3. Drain the liquid and spoon into glass jars.
4. Heat the rest of the ingredients in a saucepan until boiling.
5. Remove from heat and pour into the jars.
6. Refrigerate.

DESSERTS

No meal is complete without a selection of desserts. Most Amish and Mennonite homes always have ice cream in the freezer to accompany any of these delicious cakes and pies.

BASIC PIE CRUST

Ingredients

- 1½ cups all-purpose flour
- ¼ teaspoon fine salt
- 1 teaspoon granulated sugar
- 8 tablespoons cold unsalted butter (1 stick)
- 4 to 5 tablespoons ice water

Directions

1. Cut the butter into small pieces.
2. Combine the flour, salt, and sugar in a large bowl and stir until mixed.
3. Put the pieces of butter into the mixture and mix until the butter is coated. Using your fingers or a fork cut the butter until slightly yellow in color and in small little pieces.
4. Drizzle the ice water into mix just until the dough comes together. Less is more so do not feel as if you must use all of the ice water.
5. Shape the dough into a flat disk and press it into a pie pan. Refrigerate it for 30 minutes before using it.
6. Makes one 9-inch pie shell.*

NOTE: Dough can be frozen. Alternatively, you can use less sugar for more tart crusts.

Applesauce Cake

Ingredients

- 1 cup sugar
- ½ cup vegetable shortening
- 2 eggs
- 2 cups all-purpose flour
- 1 teaspoon ground cinnamon
- 1 teaspoon baking soda
- ½ teaspoon salt
- 1½ cups applesauce
- 1 teaspoon vanilla extract
- ½ cup chopped walnuts or pecans

Directions

1. Preheat oven to 350° F.
2. Coat a 9x13-inch baking dish with cooking spray.
3. In a large bowl, cream sugar and shortening.
4. Beat in the eggs.
5. Mix in the flour, cinnamon, baking soda, and salt.
6. Mix in the applesauce and vanilla.
7. Add the walnuts and mix well.
8. Pour batter into prepared baking dish.
9. Bake 30 to 35 minutes.

Black Walnut Layer Cake

Ingredients

- 2 ¼ cup sugar
- 3½ cup flour, sifted
- 3½ teaspoon baking powder
- 1 teaspoon salt
- 2 cup chopped black walnuts
- 1¼ cup butter
- 1¼ cup milk
- 2 teaspoons vanilla extract
- 5 eggs

Directions

1. Preheat oven to 350° F.
2. Sift the sugar, flour, baking powder and salt.
3. Cream the butter and add the eggs.
4. Beat all of the dry ingredients (except the black walnuts).
5. In a separate bowl, combine of the liquid ingredients and mix well.
6. Add half of the sifted dry ingredients to half of the milk and mix.
7. Add the remaining sifted dry ingredients, the milk and the vanilla.
8. Beat until smooth.

9. Flour 1½ cups of the chopped black walnuts and mix into the batter.
10. Grease and flour two 9-inch cake pans.
11. Pour equal amounts of batter into the two greased and floured cake pans.
12. Bake for 40-50 minutes.
13. Let cool 10 minutes, and then remove from pans.
14. After the cake has cooled, frost with buttercream icing.
15. Sprinkle remaining black walnut pieces on top of frosted cake.

BUTTERCREAM ICING

Ingredients

- ½ cup solid vegetable shortening
- ½ cup butter
- ¼ cup plus 1 tablespoon milk
- 5 cups confectioners sugar
- 1½ teaspoon vanilla or almond extract

Directions

1. Cream butter and shortening.
2. Add extract.
3. Add in the sugar and beat until icing appears dry (use a hand mixer or an electric mixer).
4. Add the milk and beat until light and fluffy.

Funny Cake

Ingredients

- 1 cup sugar
- ¼ cup lard or shortening
- 1 cup flour
- 1 teaspoon baking powder
- ¼ cup cocoa
- ¾ cup vanilla
- 1 egg
- ½ cup milk
- ⅓ cup water
- Pie shell

Directions

1. Preheat oven to 375° F.
2. In a small bowl, mix ½ cup of sugar with cocoa.
3. Add ⅓ cup hot water with ¼ teaspoon vanilla.
4. Pour into the bottom of pie shell.
5. For the top part, cream the lard before mixing in ½ cup sugar and egg until the texture is creamy.
6. In a sifter, mix the baking powder and flour.

7. In a small measuring cup, mix the milk with ½ teaspoon vanilla.

8. Alternate between sifting in the baking powder and flour mixture with the milk and vanilla mixture, pour into bottom part of pie shell.

9. Bake for 40 minutes.

NOTE: This is a Mennonite recipe. Whenever I ask the Amish about Funny Cake, they have no idea what I'm talking about. One time, I sent a Funny Cake overnight to one of my Amish friends because she didn't believe me that such a dessert existed. They loved it.

This is great with vanilla ice cream. Once you taste it, you will love, love, love it!

GROUND CHERRY PIE

Ingredients

- 2½ cups ground cherries
- ½ cup packed brown sugar
- 4 tablespoon all-purpose flour
- 2 tablespoons water
- 3 tablespoons white sugar
- 2 tablespoons butter
- Pie shell

Directions

1. Preheat oven to 450° F.
2. If not already shelled, husk the ground cherries and wash them.
3. Place the ground cherries in the pie shell. Set aside.
4. In a small bowl, mix brown sugar and 1 tablespoon flour and sprinkle over cherries.
5. Sprinkle water over top.
6. In another small bowl, mix the remaining flour and sugar.
7. Using fingers, cut butter in until crumbly. Top cherry mixture with crumbs.
8. Bake in the preheated oven for 10 minutes, reduce temperature to 350° F and continue to bake for 25 minutes.

9. Let cool before serving.

NOTE: Ground cherries are hard to find. Plan ahead and order them online if your local grocer does not stock them.

Pecan Pie

Ingredients

- ¾ stick unsalted butter
- 1¼ cups sugar, brown
- ¾ cup corn syrup (light or dark)
- 2 teaspoon pure vanilla extract
- ½ teaspoon grated orange zest
- ¼ teaspoon salt
- 3 large eggs
- 1½ to 2 cups pecan halves

Directions

1. Preheat oven to 350° F.
2. Melt butter in a small saucepan over medium heat.
3. Add brown sugar, whisking until smooth.
4. Remove from heat and whisk in corn syrup, vanilla, zest, and salt.
5. In a separate bowl, beat the eggs before adding the corn syrup mixture.
6. Put pecans in pie shell and pour corn syrup mixture evenly over them.
7. Bake on hot baking sheet until filling is set (approximately one hour).
8. Cool completely.

NOTE: You can also toast the pecans for a few minutes before adding them to the pie shell.

Pretzel Salad

Ingredients

- 2 cups crushed pretzels
- ¾ cup butter, melted
- 1 ⅛ cups white sugar
- 1 (8 ounce) package cream cheese, softened
- 1 (8 ounce) container frozen whipped topping, thawed
- 2 (3 ounce) packages strawberry gelatin mix
- 2 cups boiling water
- 2 (10 ounce) packages frozen strawberries

Directions

1. Preheat oven to 400° F.
2. Make the crust by mixing the crushed pretzels with melted butter and 3 tablespoons sugar.
3. Press the mixture into a 9 x 13 inch baking dish.
4. Bake for approximately 8 minutes and then set aside to cool.
5. In a large mixing bowl, mix the cream cheese and 1 cup sugar.
6. Fold in whipped topping. Spread mixture into the crust.
7. Dissolve gelatin in boiling water.

8. Stir in frozen strawberries and allow to set.
9. When mixture is about the consistency of egg whites, pour and spread over cream cheese layer.
10. Refrigerate until set.

NOTE: Alternatives include using raspberries, blueberries, or a mixture of the above.

Shoo-Fly Pie

Ingredients

- 1 pie shell
- 1 cup molasses (mild)
- ¾ cup hot water
- ¾ teaspoon baking soda
- 1 egg, beaten
- 1½ cups all-purpose flour
- 1 cup sugar, brown
- ¼ cup shortening

Directions

1. Preheat oven to 400° F.
2. In a medium bowl combine molasses, hot water, and baking soda. Stir well.
3. Whisk in beaten egg.
4. Pour mixture into 9-inch pie shell.
5. In a medium bowl combine flour and brown sugar.
6. Mix well, then cut in shortening until mixture resembles coarse crumbs.
7. Sprinkle on top of molasses layer.
8. Bake in preheated oven for 15 minutes.
9. Lower temperature to 350° F.
10. Bake for an additional 30 minutes.

SNITZ PIE

Ingredients

- 2 cups dried apples
- ⅔ cup sugar
- 1½ cups water
- ½ teaspoon cinnamon
- ½ teaspoon powdered cloves

Directions

1. Preheat oven to 425° F.
2. Soak apples in 1½ cups warm water and then cook apples in water in the same water.
3. When soft, push apples through a colander.
4. Add sugar and spices.
5. Put mixture in an unbaked pie shell.
6. Cover pie with top crust, fasten at edges.
7. Bake for 15 minutes.
8. Reduce temperature to 370° F and continue to bake for 35 minutes.

WEEKLY RECIPES

Be certain to follow Sarah Price's Blog (http://www.sarahpriceauthor.com) for her Friday Fare, a weekly recipe to help you jumpstart the weekend.

WANT TO CONTRIBUTE?

Do you have a special plain and simple recipe that you'd like to have added to Sarah Price's Summer Gathering's Cookbook? Feel free to email it to sarahprice.recipes@gmail.com. Please note that recipes cannot be returned and by submitting them, you acknowledge that Sarah Price is granted the necessary rights to publish them without compensation. However, all submitted recipes will be noted as having been contributed by you. If more than one person submits the same recipes, both names will be referenced as contributors.

Preorders will be available on amazon.com by December 21, 2014.

ABOUT THE AUTHOR

The Preiss family emigrated from Europe in 1705, settling in Pennsylvania as the area's first wave of Mennonite families. Sarah Price has always respected and honored her ancestors through exploration and research about her family's history and their religion. At the age of nineteen she befriended an Amish family and lived on their farm throughout the years.

Twenty-five years later Sarah Price splits her time between her home outside of New York City and an Amish farm in Lancaster County, Pennsylvania, where she retreats to reflect, write, and reconnect with her Amish friends and Mennonite family.

Contact the author by email at sarahprice.author@gmail.com. Visit her weblog at http://sarahpriceauthor.com or on Facebook at www.facebook.com/fansofsarahprice.

Made in the USA
Middletown, DE
18 January 2016